LIZARDS

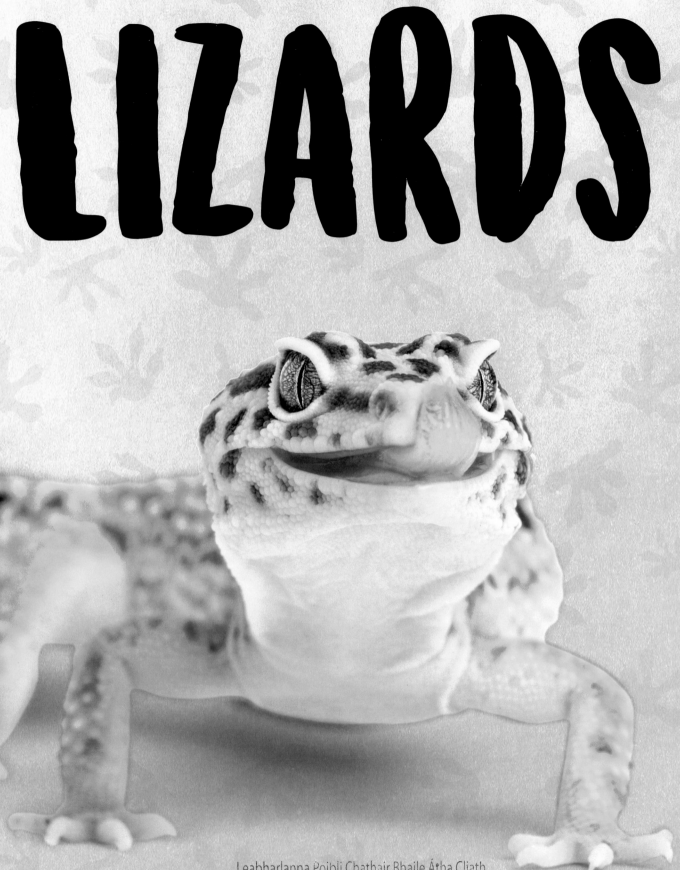

First published in Great Britain in 2019
by Wayland

Copyright © Hodder and Stoughton, 2019

Editor: Victoria Brooker
Produced for Wayland by Dynamo
Written by Pat Jacobs

MIX
Paper from
responsible sources
FSC® C104740
FSC
www.fsc.org

HBK ISBN: 978 1 5263 1001 9
PBK ISBN: 978 1 5263 1002 6

10 9 8 7 6 5 4 3 2 1

Wayland, an imprint of
Hachette Children's Group
Part of Hodder and Stoughton
Carmelite House
50 Victoria Embankment
London EC4Y 0DZ

An Hachette UK Company
www.hachette.co.uk
www.hachettechildrens.co.uk

Printed and bound in China

Picture acknowledgements:

**All images courtesy of Getty Images iStock apart from: p14
br Shutterstock**

(Key: br- bottom right)

CONTENTS

YOUR LIZARD FROM HEAD TO TAIL

Lizards are cold-blooded animals. So instead of using food as fuel to keep warm (like mammals), they rely on the heat of the sun to raise their body temperature. Cold-blooded creatures are most active when it's warm and move slowly when it's cold.

Tongue: Lizards 'smell' with their tongue, flicking it out to catch scent particles. An organ on the roof of their mouth detects the chemicals in the scent particles.

Tail: Many lizards have a weak point in their tail so if it gets caught by a predator, the lizard can run off, leaving its tail behind.

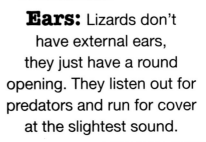

Teeth: Most lizards' teeth continue to grow all their lives. If they lose teeth, they just grow new ones!

Ears: Lizards don't have external ears, they just have a round opening. They listen out for predators and run for cover at the slightest sound.

LIZARD FACTS

Geckos are small lizards with a few unusual features. Unlike other lizards that are active during the day, geckos are nocturnal.

- Lizards see ultraviolet light, so they view the world differently and see colours and patterns that are invisible to us. This helps them to recognise other lizards and their prey.

- Cold-blooded reptiles eat less than warm-blooded mammals because they don't burn energy to stay warm. Therefore, they can live in places where food is hard to find, such as deserts, and survive for long periods without eating.

Voice: Geckos are the only lizards that communicate using sound. They chirp and click to one another and call if they're scared.

Feet: Many geckos have toe pads covered with microscopic hairs that create an electrical force similar to static electricity. This sticks their feet to surfaces and allows them to climb like Spider-Man!

Eyes: Most geckos don't have eyelids. They clean their eyes by licking them with their tongue.

BEST LIZARDS FOR BEGINNERS

Lizards are found on all continents except Antarctica, so each species has different needs when it comes to temperature, humidity and food. Make sure you know exactly how to care for your pet before you bring it home.

Crested geckos live in trees so need a tall enclosure with branches and leaves. They can be fed a meal replacement powder, so are good for owners who don't want to deal with live bugs.

Leopard geckos come in lots of colours. Unlike most geckos, they don't have sticky toe pads so they move slowly and are easy to handle. They live on the ground and eat live crickets, locusts, waxworms and silkworms.

Bearded dragons are friendly and easy to tame. They need a large tank heated to a high temperature. They eat insects, worms, baby mice, vegetables and fruit.

African fat-tailed geckos come from West Africa and make gentle, easy to handle pets. They eat live crickets, locusts, mealworms and waxworms and they also enjoy tinned dog food or defrosted baby mice!

Blue-tongued skinks are large lizards that need plenty of space. These good-natured pets eat vegetables, fruit, flowers, cooked meat and insects. They come from Australia and Indonesia and use their blue tongue to scare predators.

Uromastyx are plant-eating lizards from the Middle East and Africa. They need very hot enclosures with somewhere nice to burrow, and they can be tricky to handle. Choose a smaller species – some get very large and their tails can be dangerous!

Green anoles are active little lizards from the southeastern United States. They change colour from brown to green. They're 'hands off' pets that eat insects and don't like being handled.

IGUANAS, LARGE MONITORS AND CHAMELEONS

Iguanas and full-sized monitor lizards are intelligent and unusual pets, but they grow very big quickly. They can become aggressive as they get older, and their sharp claws, strong tail, and powerful bite, can cause serious injuries. Chameleons are fascinating, but they're not ideal pets. They don't like to be handled and need a large enclosure with perfect conditions, or they become stressed and die.

FIND YOUR PERFECT PET

Lizards are individuals with different personalities. They are intelligent creatures and are able to learn and develop good relationships with their owners. Bearded dragons are super friendly and often like to sit on their owner's lap or shoulder.

DIFFERENT DIETS

Many lizards are insectivores and need to eat live prey. If you don't fancy a tub of wriggling mealworms in your fridge or trying to keep a box of crickets alive, consider a crested gecko, a uromastyx or a skink.

HEALTH CHECK

- Lizards should be active and alert when handled.
- They should not have visible ribs or tail bones.
- Their skin should be clean, without scratches, bites or sores on the nose.
- Check for mites: tiny moving black or orange flecks on the head, neck or belly.

COUNTING THE COST

A lizard's natural home is very different to ours, and creating a safe and comfortable environment for them can be expensive. The bigger the lizard, the more you will have to spend on a tank and other equipment, so check how large your pet will grow. The cost of keeping a tank really hot adds up as well. If space is limited and you want to buy a small tank, a gecko or a green anole is a good choice.

LIFESPAN GUIDE

Lizards are long-lived pets and keep growing throughout their lives. Here's a guide to how long your lizard might live and the size it could possibly reach.

Lizard	Lifespan	Length
Bearded dragon	up to 10 years	up to 60 cm (2 ft)
Green anole	up to 8 years	up to 20 cm (8 in)
Leopard gecko	up to 20 years	up to 25 cm (10 in)
Blue-tongued skink	up to 20 years	up to 60 cm (2 ft)
Chinese water dragon	up to 15 years	up to 90 cm (3 ft)
Uromastyx	up to 15 years	up to 60 cm (2 ft)
Crested gecko	up to 20 years	up to 20 cm (8 in)
African fat-tailed gecko	up to 25 years	up to 23 cm (9 in)

Fancy a box of us living in your home?

LIZARDS ARE LONERS

Lizards are happy to live alone and see tank mates as rivals for food and the best basking spot. Males should never be kept together as they fight. If you keep a mixed pair, you may end up with more lizards than you can house, and it can be hard to find homes for unwanted babies.

Choose a lizard that's been born in captivity. Those that have been taken from the wild will be more tricky to tame and are often infected with parasites, too.

GETTING PREPARED

Do some research into how your lizard lives in the wild so you can create the perfect home for your new pal. It will take time to set up the tank and check that all the equipment is working, so don't collect your pet until everything is ready.

ROOM TO GROW

A vivarium or tank should be big enough for your lizard when it's fully grown, so find out its maximum adult size. Lizards that live on the ground, such as leopard geckos and blue-tongued skinks, need a long, wide tank, while climbers, such as crested geckos, are happier in a tall enclosure with lots of branches. Glass or plastic tanks should have a wire mesh lid so your pets have some fresh air.

FLOORING

The ideal reptile flooring (substrate) absorbs liquid and controls smells, but experts often disagree about which is best. Loose materials, such as sand or pellets, can be swallowed along with prey and cause impaction, which is a common health problem. Reptile carpet avoids this risk, but it's not as absorbent and needs regular washing. Paper or kitchen towels are cheap and convenient, but they don't look as natural.

If you use loose material on the floor of my cage I might swallow it by mistake, so please put my food in a bowl.

FURNISHING THE TANK

Lizards feel more secure if they have places to hide as they would in the wild to stay safe from predators. You should place one hidey hole on the warm side of the tank and one where it's cooler (find out about this on page 11). They need a comfortable basking spot, such as a rock or branch, underneath the heat lamp and another in the cooler part of the tank.

WATERFALLS

Some lizards won't drink from a bowl and need a moving source of water, such as a waterfall. These are attractive additions to a tank and help to raise the humidity.

ESSENTIAL EQUIPMENT

Recreating your lizard's natural environment in its new home is essential for its survival. Different species need different conditions, so check out the perfect temperature, humidity and UV light level for your pet.

HEATING

Lizards bask in the sun, so a thermostat-controlled heat lamp with a guard is the most natural source of warmth for your pet. Heat mats can crack tanks and may burn your lizard. The tank should have a warm side and a cooler side, so your pet can move around to find the perfect spot. Lizards are used to cold nights in the wild, so a timer can be used to switch off the heat lamp at night.

ULTRAVIOLET LIGHTING

Ultraviolet light is part of sunlight, but it can't pass through glass or plastic so you need a UV lamp inside your pet's enclosure. UV light is divided into types A, B and C depending on its wavelength. UVA light allows lizards to see markings on their prey that are invisible without it, which encourages them to feed. UVB light produces vitamin D3 in the skin, which keeps a lizard's bones strong. Even nocturnal geckos benefit from UV light, as they would normally be active at dawn and dusk.

HUMIDITY

Some lizards live in steamy rainforests and others come from dry deserts. Air that is too damp or too dry can put your pet's life at risk. Check out the chart on this page and get a hygrometer for inside the tank to measure the moisture level, too. You can raise the humidity by misting the enclosure once or twice a day with a spray bottle, adding a large, shallow water dish to the warm part of the tank, or changing the substrate to something that absorbs moisture, such as bark.

Lizard	Humidity	Tank temperature	Basking zone
Leopard gecko	40–60%	23–27°C (74–80°F)	30–32°C (87-90°F)
Crested gecko	70–80%	24°C (75°F)	27°C (80°F)
African fat-tailed gecko	over 50%	27°C (80°F)	32°C (90°F)
Bearded dragon	35–40%	29°C (85°F)	35–43°C (95–110°F)
Uromastyx	under 35%	27–38°C (80–100°F)	49°C (120°F) or more.
Blue-tongued skink	30–45%	24–28°C (75–82°F)	32–38°C (90–100°F)
Green anole	60–70%	24–27°C (75–80°F)	29–32°C (85–90°F)

BRINGING YOUR LIZARD HOME

Now you've created the perfect home for your lizard, it's time to collect your scaly pal. Being well prepared will help make your pet's journey, and introduction to its tank, as stress-free as possible.

PREPARING THE TANK

Put fresh water in the tank before your lizard comes home and make sure the temperature of the enclosure is suitable for your pet. On arrival, put the transport container into the tank, close to the water, and open it up. Let your lizard come out in its own time. Turn off the heat lamp for the first hour so your pet has a chance to adjust, then turn on the heat lamp and remove the travelling container.

THE JOURNEY HOME

Travelling with a reptile is more complicated than transporting other pets because you need to keep your lizard's temperature steady during the journey. In extreme weather you may need heat packs and insulation such as a blanket, or cold packs if it's hot. Your lizard will probably be in a clear plastic box. If so, cover the box with a towel as your pet will be calmer in the dark.

FEEDING YOUR NEW FRIEND

Find out when your lizard had its last meal, what it's used to eating, and how often it gets fed. Make sure that you have food for your pet for the next few days, but let it settle in before you start to feed it.

GIVE YOUR PET SOME SPACE

Don't try taming your new lizard for at least two weeks. During this time you should let your pet get to know you and look out for any signs of stress or ill health, such as hiding or not eating. Sudden noises will startle your lizard, so try to be quiet around its tank. Reptiles like routine, so it's a good idea to visit your pet at around the same time each day.

UNDERSTAND YOUR PET

Moving to a new home is stressful for me so I'll need plenty of time to settle in.

FEEDING TIME

Lizards love to eat and if you stick to a regular feeding schedule, your lizard will get excited when it sees you coming.

BUG-FREE FOOD

Not all lizards need to eat insects. Uromastyx are vegetarians and crested geckos can be fed a specially formulated meal replacement powder. While meat should make up a third of a blue-tongued skink's diet, it can be good quality dog food, canned snails or cooked chicken. They'll even eat hard-boiled eggs!

FEEDING LIVE PREY

You may not enjoy feeding insects and worms to your pet, but catching live prey is part of many lizards' natural behaviour and it enriches their lives in captivity. Use tongs or tweezers to handle live prey if you don't want to touch! Don't give your pet any prey that's larger than the distance between its eyes because it may choke, and never give your lizard more insects than it can eat. Any that are left in the tank will spread bacteria and may nibble your pet's toes, tail and eyelids.

BECOME A CRICKET KEEPER

Crickets can die if they're not immediately fed to your pet, but you can keep them alive in a large, deep plastic box with lots of small airholes in the lid. Put cardboard egg cartons and a few cardboard tubes in the box and add a jar lid filled with wet cottonwool balls so they have something to drink. You can buy 'gut-loading' cricket food to make them especially nutritious for your lizard, or feed them porridge oats and vegetables. Some crickets will hide in the tubes, so you can slide them into a plastic bag when you want to feed your pet. Cockroaches can be kept in the same way.

VITAL VITAMINS

Your pet's diet is less varied than a wild lizard's, so it will need extra calcium and vitamins to stay healthy. Most owners provide these by dusting prey in a special powder just before they feed their pets. Put some powder in a plastic bag, then add the live insects, shake the bag so they are covered in powder and tip them into your pet's tank.

UNDERSTAND YOUR PET

I need to eat fruit and vegetables as well as insects, otherwise I may get sick.

Don't feed your lizard wild insects as they may have been sprayed with pesticide and can carry diseases. Avoid giving them avocado, lettuce, spinach, acidic citrus fruits or rhubarb.

CARING FOR YOUR LIZARD

Make sure your lizard stays as healthy as possible! Check the temperature and humidity of its enclosure each day, make sure the UV lights are working, and spot clean the tank.

DEEP CLEANING

The tank and everything in it must be deep cleaned every few weeks to kill bacteria. A small holding tank is handy for keeping your pet safe while you clean. Use a reptile-safe disinfectant or mix your own using a tablespoon of washing up liquid, 30 ml (1 fl oz) of bleach and 1 litre (2 pints) of water. Wear rubber gloves and rinse everything thoroughly afterwards. Let the tank dry before putting your pet back in.

DAILY HOUSEKEEPING

Keeping your lizard's tank clean will make it a healthier place for your pet to live and stop it smelling. Lizards aren't smelly pets, but their food may smell if it's left. Spot clean the tank daily, wiping up mess, and removing uneaten food and droppings. Food and water bowls must be cleaned every day and water should be replaced.

Leopard geckos poop in one corner of the tank, so you can put a triangle of paper towel in that corner for a quick and easy clean-up.

MISTING

Some lizards, such as geckos, benefit from being sprayed with water once a day. Make sure the water isn't too cold, and give them a fine misting, so their skin is moist, but not dripping wet.

BATHING YOUR LIZARD

Some keepers bath their lizards every week – it helps to keep them hydrated. If your pet has shed its skin recently and some patches are left, baths can help to remove them. The water temperature should feel just warm on your wrist. Offer your lizard fresh water beforehand so it doesn't drink dirty bathwater!
Never bath anoles.

UNDERSTAND YOUR PET

Only give me a bath if you know I enjoy it.

HEALTH CHECK

Lizards often don't show signs of illness until they have been sick for some time, so you need to take your pet to the vet if it stops eating regularly, is thirstier than normal, starts hiding all the time, or if any parts of its body are swollen.

IMPACTION

If your lizard stops eating and pooping, it may have a blocked intestine. This is called impaction and can be deadly. You can try solving this by bathing your lizard in slightly warm water up to its shoulders for about 20 minutes. Gently massage its tummy from front to back during this time, topping up the water if it gets cold. If it still doesn't pass any droppings, take it to the vet.

CAUSES OF IMPACTION

Here are some causes of impaction and how to avoid them.

Not enough water. In the wild, lizards often get water by licking dew from leaves and not all will drink from a bowl. If your lizard isn't drinking, try misting it several times a day so it can lick the droplets from its body.

The wrong food. Omnivores, including bearded dragons and skinks, need to eat high-fibre vegetables and fruit as well as insects. Insectivores, such as geckos, should not eat too many mealworms, which are difficult to digest. Young lizards shouldn't have hard foods, such as black (field) crickets.

The wrong flooring. Sand and pellets can cause a blockage if your lizard swallows them, so try solid flooring such as carpet or paper.

Parasites. Tapeworms or roundworms can cause blockages. You may be able to see them in your lizard's droppings.

WEIGHT

Lizards store fat in their tails, so a thinner tail is often the first sign that your pet is losing weight and this can be a symptom of serious illness. Becoming overweight is just as dangerous. Weigh your pet regularly so you can spot weight loss or gain as quickly as possible.

TAIL LOSS

Some lizards shed their tail if they come under attack. The tail carries on wriggling, which distracts a predator while the lizard makes its escape. Pet lizards, including skinks and geckos, may drop their tails if they are grabbed or stepped on. The tail will grow back but it is usually shorter and a different colour. It's important to keep a lizard's tank especially clean after tail loss, so there's less chance of infection, and to feed it well because most of a lizard's fat is stored in its tail.

SALMONELLA

Reptiles can carry salmonella, which doesn't affect them but it causes stomach upsets in humans, and is especially dangerous for babies and young children. For this reason, you must always wash your hands after handling or feeding your lizard. Keep it out of rooms where food is prepared or eaten.

UNDERSTANDING YOUR LIZARD

Learning more about lizards and their natural behaviour, helps you to understand your lizard so you can give it the best possible care.

SKIN SHEDDING

A lizard's skin doesn't stretch as it grows, instead it sheds its old skin. When your pet is about to shed, it will look duller in colour and may refuse to eat. It will often be quite cranky so it's best not to handle your pet at this time. Make sure there are branches or other rough surfaces in the tank that your pet can use to rub off the loose skin and give it a shallow bowl of water to soak in. Never try to pull off pieces of skin that are stuck because you may tear the delicate new skin underneath.

DAYTIME OR NIGHTTIME PET

Most lizards are awake in the day and sleep at night, but geckos are nocturnal or crepuscular. If you'd like to spend time with your pet in the evening, a gecko is a good choice, otherwise, pick a lizard like a bearded dragon that is active in daylight.

BODY LANGUAGE

The way your lizard behaves is a clue to what it's thinking. A lizard that doesn't want to be touched will puff up, open its mouth wide, dig its claws into you or try to bite. It might also wriggle, whip its tail around or hiss. If your pet is normally tame, it may be ill or in pain, or just feeling a bit moody because it's about to shed its skin. When a lizard suddenly freezes, it's probably scared. The lizard hopes that by not moving, it won't be spotted.

BRUMATION

Brumation is the reptile equivalent of hibernation in mammals. In the wild, lizards such as bearded dragons brumate to avoid the cold and lack of food in winter. Although pet lizards have no reason to do this, their instincts sometimes tell them that they should. During this time, they may hide in the darkest part of their enclosure and not move, or eat and drink for several weeks. Your dragon may get up to drink occasionally, but don't give it food because it won't be able to digest it.

UNDERSTAND YOUR PET

I eat my old skin when I shed it so predators don't find it and come looking for me.

TAMING YOUR PET

Lizards are wild animals with lots of predators, so it's only natural that they're nervous when a human-sized creature approaches. The younger the lizard, the easier it will be to tame, but you will still need plenty of patience as it can take months before your pet is comfortable being handled.

THE WAY TO A LIZARD'S HEART

Start to bond with your pet by feeding it. Just put the food in the tank at first, then, as your pet begins to associate you with a tasty treat, use tweezers or tongs to feed it directly. Once your lizard is coming over to take food from you, try feeding it by hand. Don't touch your pet at this stage – trying to handle your lizard before it is ready will just slow things down.

LET YOUR LIZARD MAKE THE FIRST MOVE

The next step is to put your hand in the cage and let the lizard come to you. Wash your hands first if you've been touching its food, otherwise it might bite you by mistake. If your pet is ready, it will start exploring your hand and may even climb up your arm. Always approach your pet at a time of day when it's naturally active. No animal is happy when it's just been woken up from a deep sleep.

UNDERSTAND YOUR PET

I may be frightened if you suddenly grab me from above because that's what birds of prey do.

CATCHING YOUR PET

There will be times when you have to catch your lizard to move it. If your lizard won't climb onto your hand, the best way to do this is to keep your hand flat, with your fingers together, place your hand over your lizard's back and curl your fingers and thumb around its body. It may be easier to catch a large lizard in a pillowcase.

TOP TIPS

Use these handy hints to build a great friendship with your lizard!

- Although your lizard should get to know the whole family, it's best that just one person tries to tame it at first.

- Make sure the room is lizard-proof whenever the enclosure is open. Lizards move very fast and can easily escape.

- Never grab a lizard by the tail. Some lizards can detach their tails if they are caught by a predator and it might break off.

- Some people say that putting something you have worn, such as a sock, in your lizard's tank will help it to get used to your scent.

- Always wash your hands before and after handling your pet.

- Once your lizard is tame, you must keep spending time with it, otherwise it will forget you.

CREATE A COOL HOME FOR YOUR PET

In the wild, lizards have plenty to keep them busy so you should try to make their enclosure as interesting as possible, otherwise they may get bored.

DECORATIVE ROCKS

Rocks give your tank a natural look and they absorb heat. Choose rocks without sharp edges and clean them with a stiff brush, then boil them in water for 30 minutes. Don't pile rocks on top of each other in case they fall and injure your lizard.

CLIMBING AND HIDING

Branches are great for climbing, basking and hiding in, and your lizard can rub against them to remove stubborn patches of skin when it's shedding. If you take wood from the wild, strip off the bark and wash the branch in water. Dry it thoroughly and bake it in a hot oven for 30 minutes. This will kill any bugs, eggs or bacteria that might harm your pet.

PLANTS

A living plant makes a tank look more natural and attractive, while helping to raise the humidity and improving the air quality. They give your pet somewhere to hide and climb, and some lizards like to lick water from the leaves. Suitable plants include weeping fig, peace lily, spider plant, begonia, small palms and juniper. Artificial plants are also useful for hiding and climbing, and you can wash them, but beware – young lizards may mistake them for the real thing and swallow a piece of plastic.

MAKE A BASKING HAMMOCK

You will need:
- a square of fabric that fits the corner of the tank when folded in half diagonally to make a triangle. It should be big enough for your lizard to stretch out on.

- 3 round button suction cups

- some thin string or strong thread

Fold the fabric in half to make a triangle shape and tie the three corners to the suction cups. Use the suction cups to attach the hammock to the sides of your lizard's tank.

LIZARD QUIZ

By now you should know lots of things about lizards.

Test your knowledge by answering these questions.

1 How do most geckos clean their eyes?

a. By blinking
b. With their feet
c. With their tongue

2 Which of these lizards is a vegetarian?

a. Uromastyx
b. Leopard gecko
c. Green anole

3 How long does a crested gecko live?

a. Up to 8 years
b. Up to 12 years
c. Up to 20 years

4 What does a hygrometer measure?

a. Heat
b. Humidity
c. Light

5 Which of these vegetables is not good for lizards?

a. Carrot
b. Avocado
c. Broccoli

6 Which of these lizards is nocturnal?

    a. Bearded dragon
    b. Skink
    c. Crested gecko

10 Why should you remove any uneaten insects from the tank?

    a. They may nibble your lizard
    b. They spread bacteria
    c. Both of these

7 Why should you never grab your lizard by the tail?

    a. It may bite you
    b. Its tail may come off
    c. It will hurt your pet

8 What is brumation?

    a. The equivalent of hibernation
    b. A disease that affects lizards
    c. Skin shedding

9 What is the maximum size of prey you should feed to your lizard?

    a. No larger than its tail
    b. No larger than the space between its eyes
    c. No longer than half its length

QUIZ ANSWERS

1 How do most geckos clean their eyes?

   c. With their tongue

2 Which of these lizards is a vegetarian?

   a. Uromastyx

3 How long does a crested gecko live?

   c. Up to 20 years

4 What does a hygrometer measure?

   b. Humidity

5 Which of these vegetables is not good for lizards?

   b. Avocado

6 Which of these lizards is nocturnal?

   c. Crested gecko

7 Why must you never grab your lizard by the tail?

   b. Its tail may come off

8 What is brumation?

   a. The equivalent of hibernation

9 What is the maximum size of prey you should feed to your lizard?

   b. No larger than the space between its eyes

10 Why should you remove any uneaten insects from the tank?

   c. Both of these

GLOSSARY

aggressive – Likely to attack.

bacteria – Microscopic living things that are found everywhere. Some are dangerous and cause diseases, while others are helpful and keep animals healthy.

basking – Standing under a heat lamp or in the sun to warm up.

bleach – A liquid cleaner that contains chlorine and kills bacteria. It removes the colour from fabrics, so should be handled with care.

calcium – A chemical that keeps bones and teeth strong.

crepuscular – Active at dawn and dusk.

environment – The surroundings where animals live.

gut-loading – Feeding prey animals on special foods to make them more nutritious.

humidity – The amount of moisture in the air.

hydrated – Having enough water in the body.

hygrometer – An instrument that measures humidity.

impaction – A blockage in the digestive system.

insectivores – Animals that eat insects.

misting – Spraying with water.

nocturnal – Active at night.

parasite – An animal that lives in or on another creature and feeds from it (often by sucking its blood).

pesticide – Chemicals that kill insects.

predator – An animal that hunts and eats other creatures.

reptile carpet – A soft, washable carpet that can be used instead of sand or gravel on the bottom of the tank.

substrate – The material, often gravel or sand, on the floor of a tank.

ultraviolet (UV) light – Light that makes up about 10% of sunlight and is divided into UVA, UVB and UVC. Humans cannot see UV light but lizards can. Some have patterns that reflect UVA light and help them to recognise each other. UVB light produces vitamin D3 in the body, which is important for good health. Most UVC rays do not reach Earth.

vitamin D3 – A vitamin that is created in the body by sunlight and helps animals to absorb calcium.

vivarium – An enclosure for keeping pets that recreates their natural environment.

INDEX